The funfair

Written by Gillian Liu
Illustrated by Jane Green

Evans

Evans Brothers Limited

food   roundabout   sausage   plane   lollipop

The funfair was in town.
There were lots of rides to enjoy...

car

crisps

drink

toothpaste

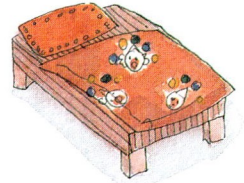
bed

and lots of food to eat.
Jake felt hungry.

food   roundabout   sausage   plane   lollipop

Jake and his sister went on a
roundabout, round and round,

car

crisps

drink

toothpaste

bed

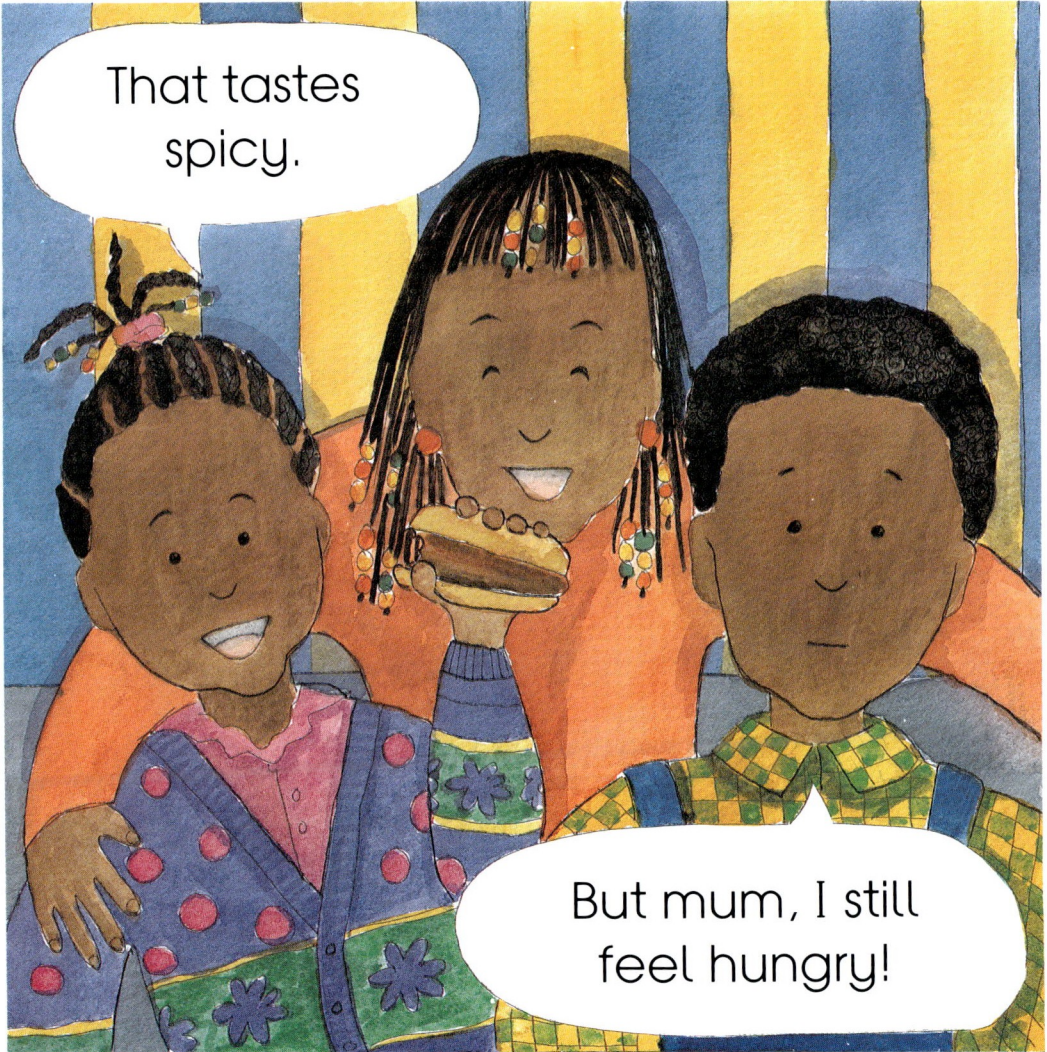

and then ate a sausage
in a roll.

food   roundabout   sausage   plane   lollipop

They went on a plane,
high and low,

car

crisps

drink

toothpaste

bed

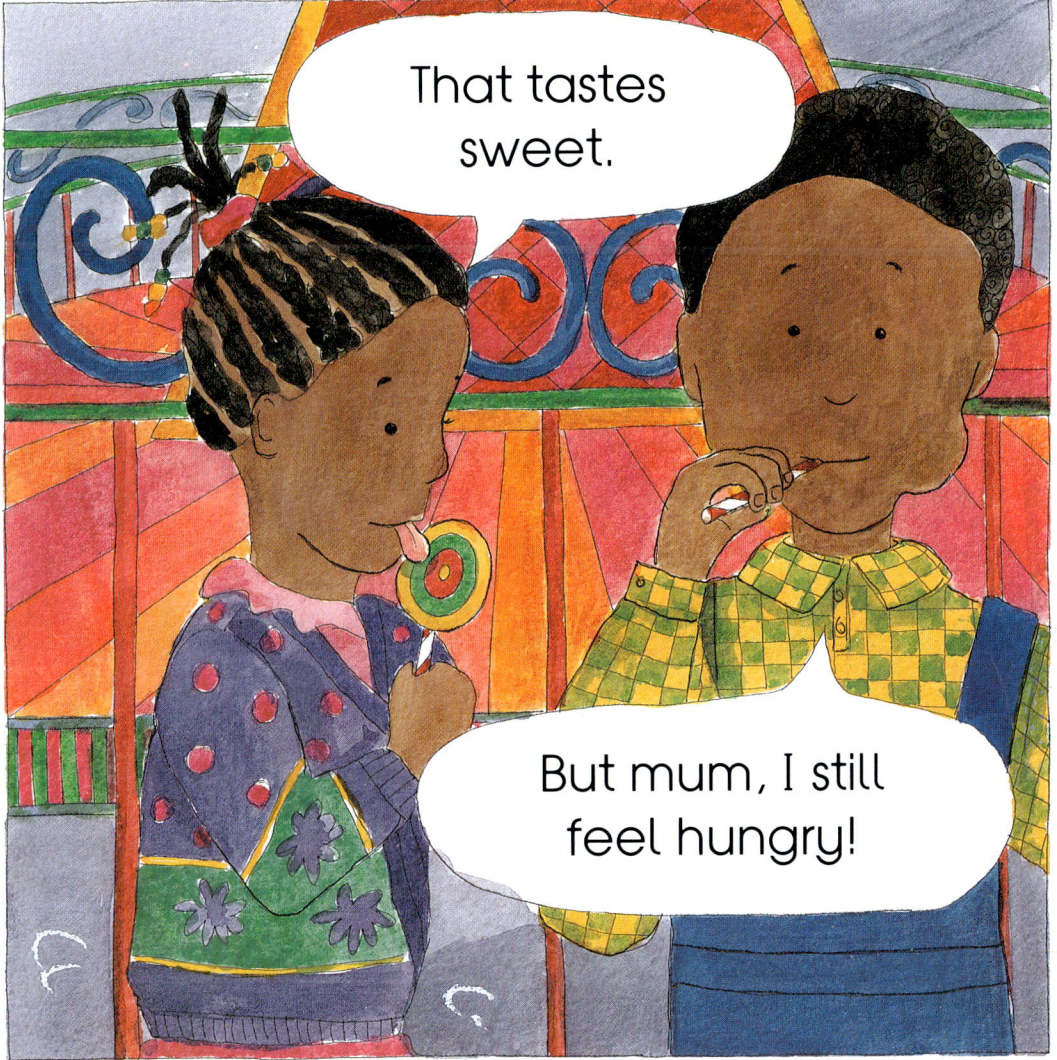

and then ate a lollipop
on a stick.

food   roundabout   sausage   plane   lollipop

They went on a dodgem car,
bumpety bump,

 car
 crisps
 drink
 toothpaste
 bed

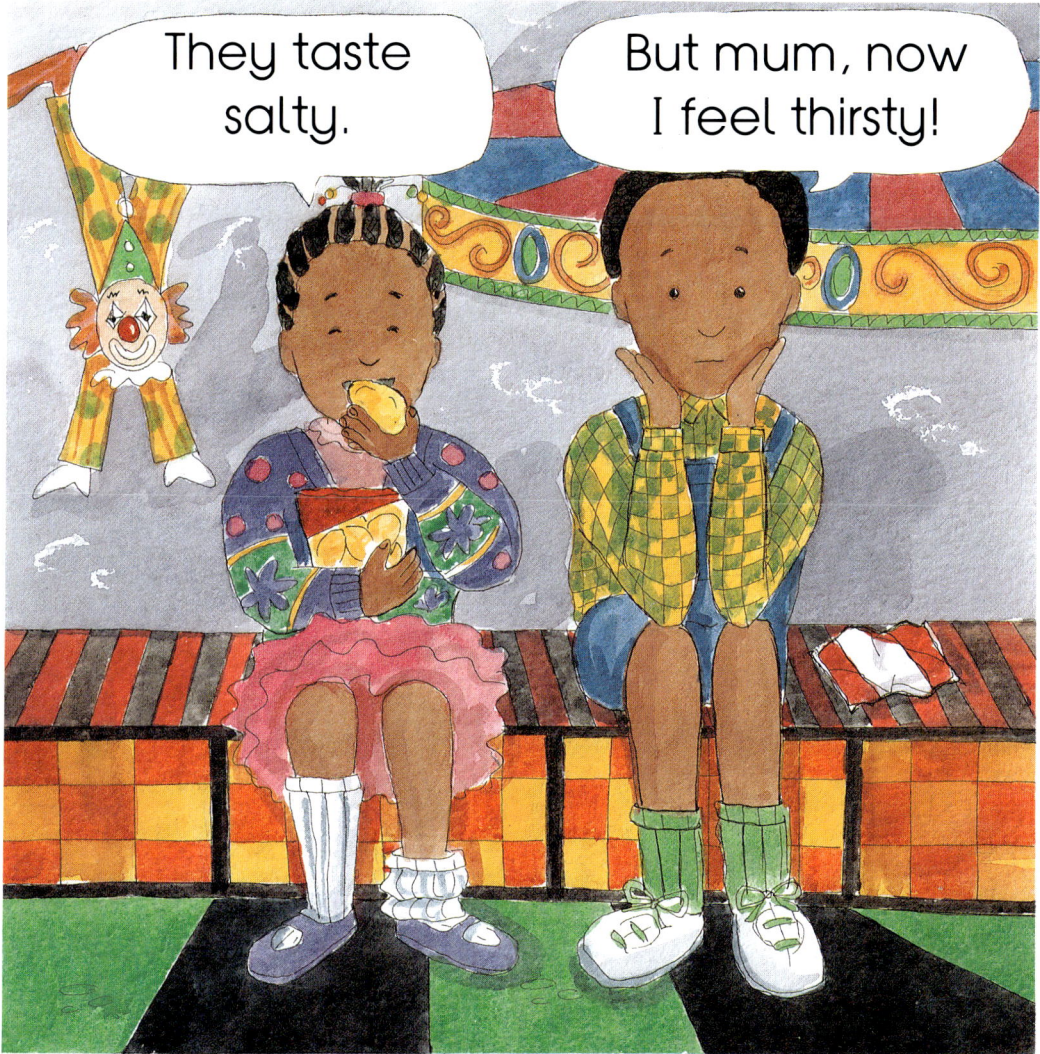

and then ate a bag of crisps.

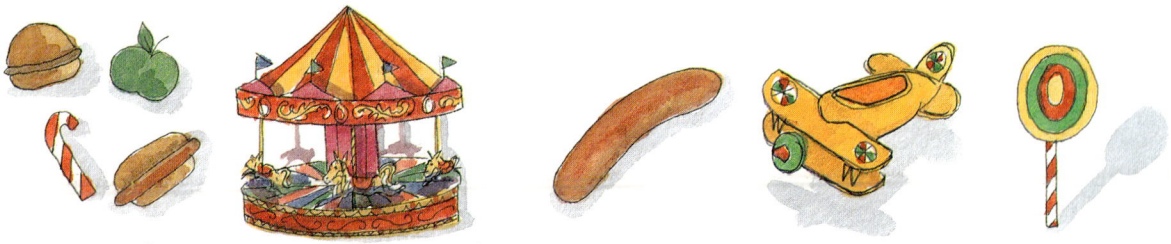

food roundabout sausage plane lollipop

That tastes
fruity.

I don't feel hungry
any more, but mum...

They went to a café
and had a drink with a straw.

car

crisps

drink

toothpaste

bed

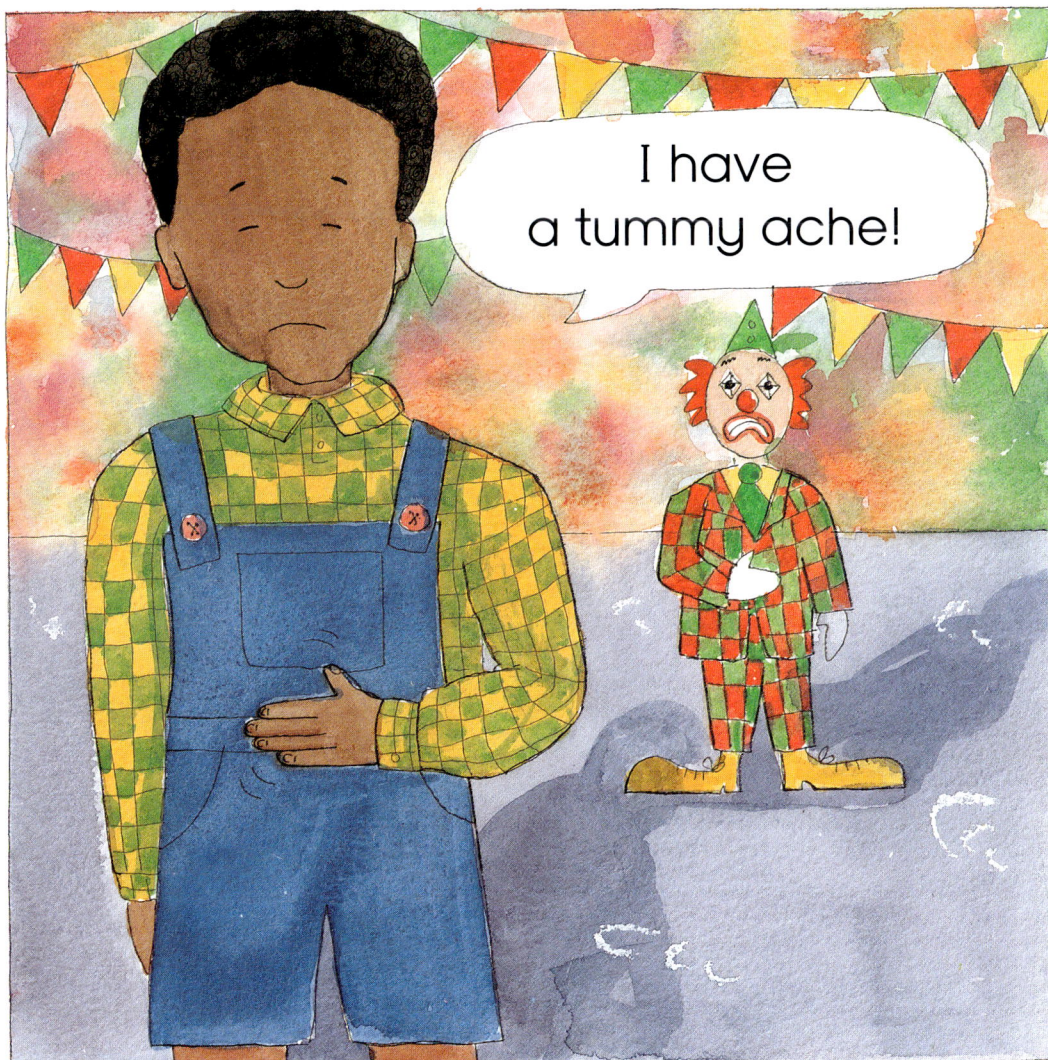

Jake did not look well.
So they all went home.

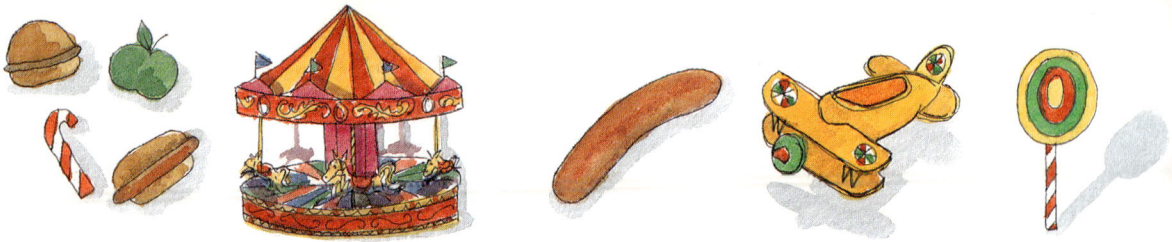

food roundabout sausage plane lollipop

Mum said there was one thing
left to taste that day.

car

crisps

drink

toothpaste

bed

Can you guess what it was?

food   roundabout   sausage   plane   lollipop

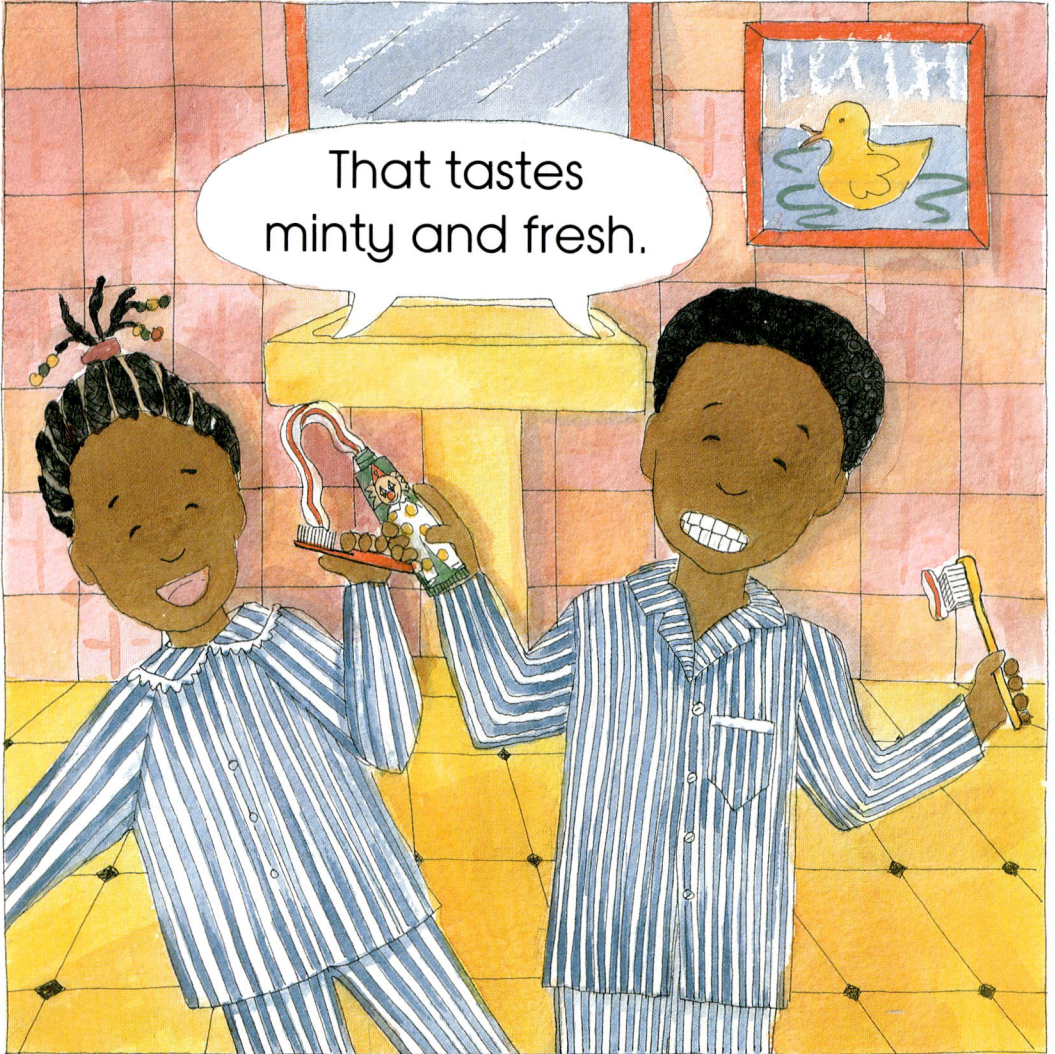

That tastes minty and fresh.

It was toothpaste!

car

crisps

drink

toothpaste
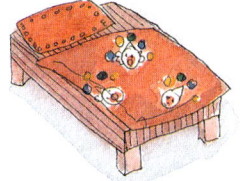
bed

Then it was time for bed.

Activities — Make some biscuits to taste

What you need

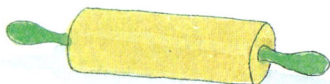

rolling pin

cheese grater

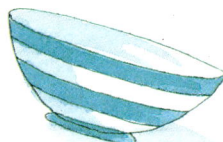

mixing bowl

teaspoon

wooden spoon

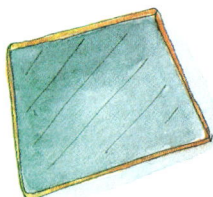

baking tray

Ingredients

90g cheese

125g plain flour

1/2 teaspoon salt

90g butter

1 egg

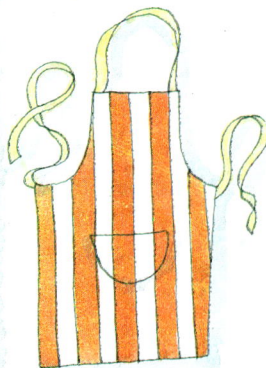

apron

sieve

cutters

scales

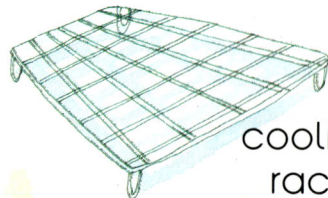

cooling rack

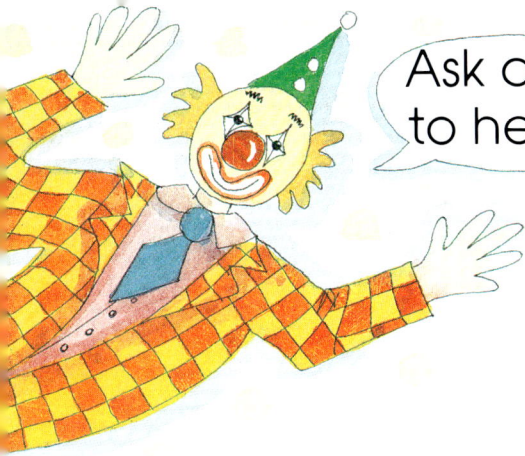

Ask an adult to help you.

What to do

1 Wash your hands.

2 Grate the cheese.

3 Sift the flour and salt in the bowl.

4 Rub the butter into the flour.

5 Add the egg.
6 Turn on the oven to gas mark 6 electricity 175°C

7 Roll out the mixture.

8 Cut out the biscuits. Put them on a baking tray.

9 Bake for 10-15 minutes. Cool the biscuits on a cooling rack.

Opposites

Can you find any clowns in the story?
Look back and see.

open   closed

happy   sad

light

heavy

big   small

front   back

fat   thin

high

long   short

full   empty

low

What time is it?

7 o'clock

8 o'clock

supper time

breakfast time

tea time

lunch time

6 o'clock

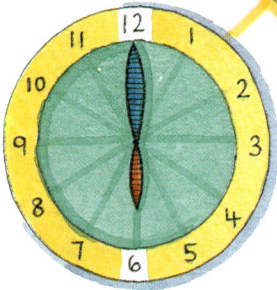

12 o'clock

What time do you eat?